Alison,

Fer Feck Sake
take more time
for You!

Feck Stress
Wherever You
Can
Love Ya Sis!

F*CK

stress

An Hachette UK Company
www.hachette.co.uk

Vie Books, an imprint of Summersdale Publishers Ltd
Part of Octopus Publishing Group Limited
Carmelite House
50 Victoria Embankment
LONDON
EC4Y 0DZ
UK

www.summersdale.com

Printed and bound in China

ISBN: 978-1-78783-009-7

Substantial discounts on bulk quantities of Summersdale books are available to corporations, professional associations and other organizations. For details contact general enquiries: telephone: +44 (0) 1243 771107 or email: enquiries@summersdale.com.

F*CK

stress

Tips and Advice on How to Banish
Anxiety from Your Life

ALEX MARTIN

INTRODUCTION

Stress sucks. From the minor irritations to the big daunting responsibilities... can't they all just f*ck off? Well, no. Stress can't f*ck off entirely, but you can change how much it gets to you by working on resilience, self-care and cultivating a no-f*cks-given attitude.

No matter what the circumstances are, everyone gets stressed every now and again. A bit of stress can be useful, however; it helps you to prioritize and keeps you motivated. In fact, without a healthy amount of stress it would be hard to do anything productive at all. We'd be in our PJs all day, ignoring bills and eating frozen yoghurt. But stress that sticks around and brings you down is detrimental to your health and well-being, causing potentially harmful health issues like high blood pressure, fatigue, depression and anxiety.

Stress will always be a part of life, but you have the power to change the way you respond to it, and how much it affects you. Read on for a veritable smorgasbord of genius ideas to help you take control and make stress your b*tch.

YOU DON'T HAVE
TO CONTROL YOUR
THOUGHTS. YOU JUST
HAVE TO STOP LETTING
THEM CONTROL YOU.

DAN MILLMAN

Write a to-do list

Instead of worrying about what you need to do, write a list of your priorities and stick to them by creating realistic deadlines. These will include lists of what needs doing today, this week, this month... as well as long-term goals. Once you have completed a task, cross it off your list and take a moment to congratulate yourself. By transferring your chores and goals from your mind to paper, you will instantly feel less pressurized and, in turn, more productive. Try keeping a running log in your journal of any achievements or milestones that feel significant to you. Look back on this list whenever you doubt yourself.

F*CK

perfection.

BEING NEGATIVE
ONLY MAKES A
DIFFICULT JOURNEY
MORE DIFFICULT.
YOU MAY BE GIVEN
A CACTUS, BUT
YOU DON'T HAVE
TO SIT ON IT.

JOYCE MEYER

Think Positively

Choosing a positive outlook over a negative one isn't always easy, but it'll reduce your stress levels dramatically. The key is to look for abundance everywhere. For example, if you catch yourself worrying that there isn't enough of something, tell yourself there is always more. You can apply it to anything: money, friends, inspiration, love, time, donuts... the list is endless. Perhaps your friend gets a great new job, while you're still looking. You can either sulk and stew in jealousy, seeing one less job available to you... or you can cheer for your friend, appreciating the undeniable proof that jobs are indeed out there and your peers are being offered them. The situation hasn't changed, but you now have a calmer, more positive way of looking at it.

STOP COMPARING YOURSELF TO OTHERS

This one's a biggie. When we fail and even when we succeed, it's human nature to look for someone who's doing better than us and find ourselves lacking in comparison. Or we might be feeling down on ourselves and look for someone doing worse than us, for an ego-boost that quickly fades. Thinking less of someone else does not improve your situation, nor does feeling inadequate make you inadequate.

Try to recognize when you compare yourself to others – but, and this is very important, under no circumstances must you beat yourself up about it. We all do it. Simply remind yourself that we all have different hurdles, skill sets and privileges. Life is not a competition, there's plenty of happiness out there for everyone.

RELEASE THE STRESS. YOU WERE NEVER IN CONTROL ANYWAY.

Set intentions and act upon them

Instead of dreaming and planning and wondering about what you might achieve, change your mindset and decide what you intend to achieve. Once you've set an intention, take small steps toward it, and don't get distracted by anything that'll take you away from your intended goal.

For example, if you intend to write a novel, start with one page – a sustainable and achievable goal you can aim for every day. Let go of any procrastination, self-doubt and comparison that might arise. Say yes to reading widely, meeting other writers and seeking inspiration. Keep writing your one page per day and in just one year you'll have a 365-page first draft of a novel. Whatever your intention, focusing on steady progress in the right direction will get you there sooner than you thought possible.

"NO"

IS A COMPLETE SENTENCE.

SAY WHAT YOU MEAN

It can be scary to tell the truth sometimes, especially if it means disagreeing with others. Agreeing and conforming often feels much more comfortable.

But pleasing others in this way often leads to us taking on too much, doing things we don't really want to do and denying our own feelings, all of which lead to increased stress.

Next time you give your opinion or take on something new, take a moment to quickly check in with yourself before speaking up... what's your gut telling you? Go with that.

You'll respect yourself and others will respect you too... and if they don't? F*ck 'em.

You probably wouldn't

WORRY

about what people

THINK

of you if you could know how

SELDOM

they do!

OLIN MILLER

CELEBRATE EVERY ACHIEVEMENT

Exercised this week? Good job! Asserted yourself at work? You're an amazing badass warrior! Resisted pettiness and took the high road? Gold f*cking star!

Everyone struggles with different things, so what might look easy on the outside can be a big challenge. It's OK to feel proud of yourself if an accomplishment is significant for you, even if it might seem small to others. Even when you stumble you can learn from your setbacks and look for progress in your reactions.

Allow yourself to celebrate the quirky personal hurdles that only make sense to you – they're a big deal!

F*CK
THE PAST
AND THE
FUTURE —
LIVE IN THE
MOMENT.

TIDY UP

This sounds like another chore to add to your to-do list, right? And sometimes, it is... but tidying up can be so much more. Choose a corner, a shelf, a cupboard – nothing too ambitious – and empty it. Move anything that doesn't belong there. Recycle, give away or throw away anything you no longer want or need. Clean the surfaces, then put everything that's left back. Mmm, satisfying.

Just looking at that spotless, organized space will lower your stress levels, because a calm environment is more conducive to a calm mind. Having clutter in your environment will stress you out every time you see it because you know it represents a task that needs doing. Plus, the act of cleaning and tidying gets you out of your head, naturally reducing stress while you work.

GENTLENESS IS STRENGTH UNDER CONTROL. IT IS THE ABILITY TO STAY CALM, NO MATTER WHAT HAPPENS.

ELIZABETH GEORGE

*Eat your f*cking greens*

Research is finding more and more evidence linking nutrition and mental health. It makes sense – the brain is a part of your body just like the heart or liver, so a well-nourished body is more able to support a healthy, resilient mind. It's also estimated that 90 per cent of the body's "happiness chemical" serotonin is made in the gut.

When we're stressed out, it's tempting to reach for comfort food, a lot of which raises blood-sugar levels, making us feel even more stressed.

Take a look at your diet and try adding more fibre-rich fruit, veg and whole grains to help keep you feeling full for longer and feed your existing gut bacteria. The more diverse your gut bacteria, the better, and fermented food and drink such as live yoghurt, sauerkraut, miso and kombucha equal party time for your intestines. A healthy gut will help regulate your mood, fight diseases and lower blood-sugar levels.

You'll never please everyone, so please

YOURSELF.

Exercise

Regular exercise is hugely beneficial to both physical and mental health – exercising daily can reduce stress levels by up to 40 per cent. The key is to find a form of exercise that you really, truly enjoy. When you look forward to exercise, it stops being a chore and you're more likely to do it on a regular basis.

By staying calm,
you increase your
resistance against
any kind of storms.

MEHMET MURAT ILDAN

STOP BEING "THE CHASER"

Stressing over why someone hasn't responded to you is a waste of time and repeatedly chasing them about it is doubly so. If they want to get back to you, they will in their own time. If you really need an answer, send one follow-up message and then leave it. Be satisfied that you have done everything you can and let go of the responsibility, knowing the ball is in their court.

GO

WITH
THE FLOW.

IGNORE YOUR PHONE

When did it start being OK for a little rectangle to constantly interrupt you with various beeps, trills and buzzes whatever the time of day, or night? How rude, how stressful! Switching off push notifications, using airplane mode or – gasp – turning it off altogether will let you concentrate on the task at hand – including a decent night's sleep. When your attention isn't constantly pulled away, you'll be able to calmly concentrate on what you're doing – be that writing an email, having a conversation or eating a slice of cake in peace.

WANNA FLY,
YOU GOT
TO GIVE UP
THE SH*T
THAT WEIGHS
YOU DOWN.

TONI MORRISON

WHOLE-ASS IT, DON'T HALF-ASS IT

Do your best, always. Your best will be different from one day to the next – sometimes you're on top of the world and capable of anything, but other days you might be ill or just not feeling 100 per cent.

Check in with yourself regularly – if you're saying yes to everything are you doing it because you want to, or are you over-extending yourself to keep others happy? Giving your whole ass to one thing you feel passionate about is way better than running yourself ragged committing to a bunch of less-than-inspiring projects. You're allowed to be picky with your time and energy, so give only as much as you want to.

If you're confident that you've done your best, you'll avoid unnecessary regret, stress and self-criticism.

Swap sorry for thank you

Apologies are sometimes necessary, but save them for when you've actually done something wrong and feel genuinely sorry. Otherwise, whenever you feel the impulse to say "sorry", take a moment and see if you can acknowledge the other person's effort rather than your own perceived shortcomings.

Swap:

- "Sorry for the late reply" for "Thanks for your text!"
- "Sorry to bother you" for "Thanks for your time."
- "Sorry for rambling" for "Thank you for listening."

Replacing a negative word with a positive one will make you feel calmer and more confident, plus the person you're thanking will feel appreciated. Win–win!

IF WE LEARN TO OPEN
OUR HEARTS, ANYONE,
INCLUDING THE PEOPLE
WHO DRIVE US CRAZY,
CAN BE OUR TEACHER.

PEMA CHÖDRÖN

ORGANIZE YOUR WARDROBE

Getting dressed in the morning doesn't need to be a mad hunt for something to wear – all it takes is a bit of organizing.

If something doesn't fit give it away, donate it to a charity shop or stick it on eBay. The same applies for clothes you haven't worn in 18 months. If it's out of season, store it somewhere away from your in-season clothes. Ripped or damaged clothes can be repaired, recycled or repurposed as cleaning rags or fabric scraps. Ta-da! You'll be left with only the clothes that you're actually likely to wear, which makes getting dressed in the morning a lot less stressful.

Chuck it in the

**F*CK-IT
BUCKET**

and move on.

GIVE YOURSELF A F*CKING PEP TALK

Everyone's inner critic is a different brand of meanie, so try a few different affirmations on for size. If it makes your self-esteem bloom, that's the one for you.

Try these stress-relieving affirmations: *I am enough, I deserve happiness, I can take a break, I love myself, I can do this!* Say your preferred affirmation to yourself whenever you feel moved to – in front of the mirror, at the start of the day, when you go to bed, and especially when you feel stressed or emotionally drained. If you make a habit of saying encouraging words to yourself, soon enough you'll start believing them and be feeling more positive, calm and in control of your life.

WHEN THERE IS NO STRUGGLE, THERE IS NO STRENGTH.

TREAT

[

THE
OBSTACLES AS
OPPORTUNITIES.

UNFRIEND WITHOUT GUILT

You know the one. There's just something about their social media posts that sends your irritation levels through the roof. Perhaps they have hurt you in the past or you can't help but compare your life to theirs... or maybe they're just blessed with a naturally infuriating personality.

Whatever the reason, you need no more justification than your own sanity to unfollow, unfriend or even block them. Your newsfeed, your rules.

TAKE A DEEP

F*CKING
BREATH.

Identify your stress "tells"

Next time you feel really stressed, notice what your body is doing. Some people clench their jaw, others might chain-smoke.

When we perform the actions that our mind associates with stress, it elicits a stress response in the brain. So, acting stressed leads to feeling stressed, and vice-versa, creating a vicious (and very stressed-out) circle!

Noticing and gently stopping your stressed-out behaviours will stop the mind and body feeding off each other and help snap you out of a stress spiral.

Even once you're aware of your stress tells, it can be really hard to snap out of it. Try distracting yourself with a bit of square breathing: picture a square, and imagine your breath tracing its edges one by one. Breathe in for the count of four, out for the count of four, in for the count of four, out for the count of four. Once your attention is focused on your breath, you can ride out the urge to perpetuate your stress.

FOR FAST-ACTING
RELIEF, TRY
SLOWING DOWN.

JANE WAGNER

STOP TAKING THINGS PERSONALLY

Nothing anyone else does is really about you... and the same goes for your own actions. They're a reflection of what's going on in your mind and how you feel about yourself.

Projection is a powerful thing, and each one of us walks around with a whole brain-full of experiences, prejudices and insecurities that colour how we see and interact with the world.

Next time you feel upset or offended by someone's actions, take a step back. This isn't about being a doormat or putting up with being treated badly: if you've been genuinely wronged, it's OK to assert yourself, walk away or both. If they've simply touched a nerve, examine your emotions around it, you might be surprised by what you find.

Good enough is

**GOOD
ENOUGH.**

GIVE YOURSELF A GIFT

Treat yourself in big and small ways that are within your budget. You get all the warm and fuzzy feelings of giving and receiving, and you deserve nice things! You could buy yourself a bunch of flowers, a slice of cake or that book you've been meaning to read.

Alternatively, give yourself gifts that money can't buy – 5 minutes to stare out of the window, an early night or letting go of an unnecessary commitment... if you start to view all pleasurable, healthy or stress-relieving actions as gifts, you can treat yourself every day!

WHAT LIES

behind us and what lies

BEFORE US

are tiny matters

COMPARED TO

what lies

WITHIN US.

HENRY S. HASKINS

Slow the f*ck down!

Being busy makes us feel important, needed and productive. Multitasking is seen as a valuable and useful skill. But is it really?

When we switch between tasks, our brains struggle with accessing different neural pathways. This can lead to mistakes and a slowing down of productivity and competence levels. Multitasking is also less conducive to creativity and causes inordinate stress when you have to keep tabs on several things at once.

Studies show the most efficient way to get things done is by completing one task at a time.

When you concentrate carefully and deliberately on one thing, your brain can "turn off" any modes of thinking not needed for the task in hand, leading to a less stressful, distraction-free way of working.

Difficult roads often lead to beautiful destinations. The best is yet to come.

ZIG ZIGLAR

LISTEN TO SOME F*CKING WHALE SONG

OK, it doesn't need to be whale song. Make a playlist of whatever type of music makes you feel relaxed, happy and like the confident, capable badass you truly are, then listen to it when you need to unwind or switch off from the world. Every time you listen to your calming playlist in order to relax, your brain will strengthen its connection between those particular songs and the feeling of relaxation.

AND NOW THAT YOU DON'T HAVE TO BE PERFECT, YOU CAN BE GOOD.

JOHN STEINBECK

Get up earlier

Start by setting your alarm just 5 minutes earlier than normal. Even 5 extra minutes in the morning can make your routine feel so much more relaxed. If you're already playing catch-up and rushing through your morning routine, this is likely to set the tone for the rest of the day. These 5 extra minutes will give you a little wiggle room between your shower, breakfast and getting out of the door so you can take your time and any unforeseen delays won't throw your whole day out of whack.

For an even less stressful morning, think about what you can do before you go to bed. Even laying out your clothes or having your coffee mug out on the worktop makes a difference.

AVOID NEGATIVE F*CKERS

We all have off-days, when we feel the world is against us and we need to vent to a friend. There's absolutely nothing wrong with that. But there are some people who are consistently negative, who manage against all odds to find the bad in everything... that sh*t's contagious, and you don't need it in your life. Try limiting the time you spend with them and see how the stress falls away.

If, however, the negative person that springs to mind is you, don't be too hard on yourself. You have the power to change, but you can't bully yourself into a positive mindset. Simply noticing your habits is the first step to changing them. Try journaling about your own habits around negativity, to see if you can unpick your thought processes and shift your mindset to a more positive one.

FAILURE IS ONLY
THE OPPORTUNITY TO
BEGIN AGAIN MORE
INTELLIGENTLY.

HENRY FORD

Ask for help

You are not a burden to your colleagues, friends or loved ones. If you're feeling overwhelmed, reach out to those around you. Can you delegate a stressful task or collaborate with someone else, pooling your skills? Even if it feels like your stress is really obvious and people are ignoring it, no one can read your mind! Most people will be happy to lend a hand if asked.

You are a

MAGNIFICENT

shiny-ass beast.

SPEND TIME WITH ANIMALS

Studies have found that just being around animals lowers blood pressure and heart rate, as well as reducing stress and anxiety. Stroking a cat, talking to a rabbit, walking a dog or hugging a llama whenever you get the chance is a great way to de-stress, and the animal will enjoy it too.

If you don't have a furry friend handy, don't worry. Several studies have found that even viewing cute animal videos online has a stress-reducing effect.

RULE NUMBER ONE IS, DON'T SWEAT THE SMALL STUFF. RULE NUMBER TWO IS, IT'S ALL SMALL STUFF.

ROBERT ELIOT

Accept everything as if you had chosen it

It's easy for stress levels to rise when a spanner is thrown in the works of your morning routine or a carefully planned project. Take a leaf out of spiritual teacher Eckhart Tolle's book: "Whatever the present moment contains, accept it as if you had chosen it."

Acceptance doesn't mean you have to like your situation, it doesn't mean you can't work to change it and it definitely doesn't mean you deserve any sh*t you're having to deal with. Acceptance means letting go of torturing yourself imagining ways things could have turned out differently.

Hard as it may be, you can learn from any challenge, and you can make use of any delay.

Try it for one day and see if you notice a difference. Act as if you chose everything: the traffic jam and the spilled coffee as well as the free chocolate bar from the vending machine.

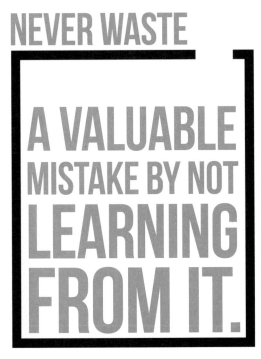

NEVER WASTE

A VALUABLE MISTAKE BY NOT LEARNING FROM IT.

GET COMFY WITH BEING A BEGINNER

You don't need to be an expert on everything, and there's no way of knowing what you haven't yet learned. Each day brings with it a totally unique set of circumstances and challenges – like taking on new responsibilities at work, or navigating a change in your relationship status – and it's OK not to know exactly what you're doing. Be open to learning and asking questions – and tell that inner critic to shut the hell up.

THE GREATEST
WEAPON AGAINST
STRESS IS OUR
ABILITY TO CHOOSE
ONE THOUGHT
OVER ANOTHER.

WILLIAM JAMES

Get silly

Play is one of the most powerful stress-relievers, but as adults we just don't play enough! The fear of looking awkward or silly stops many of us from having fun just for the hell of it.

Try ignoring the thought that you're too old for play – roll down a hill, learn a dance routine on YouTube, bounce on a trampoline, build some Lego, doodle, play with a pet – do whatever feels good for the sake of feeling good.

CHOOSE HAPPINESS.

IF YOU TREAT

every situation as a

LIFE AND DEATH

matter, you'll die a lot of

TIMES.

DEAN SMITH

F*ck what other people think!

Imagining how you're seen by others piles a bunch of needless pressure on yourself. We're often our own worst critics, so it's easy to assume everyone is judging your actions and finding you lacking. Here's the truth: you have literally no idea what or how much other people think of you. Plus, it's really none of your business! Work out whose opinions you actually value (hint: this will be those who know and love you best) and let go of the need to control or understand anyone else's. As long as your actions make sense to you, no one else matters.

**The time to relax
is when you don't
have time for it.**

SYDNEY J. HARRIS

ASSERT YOUR BOUNDARIES

Boundaries are about learning where you end and others begin. Protect your boundaries by being assertive with the things you can control – your responses, your time, your actions and the effort you put in. For example, in order to ensure a healthy work–life balance you might not check work emails outside of office hours, or maybe you choose to eat lunch by yourself. Being clear with yourself and others about what's important to you and what you will and won't accept might feel uncomfortable at first, but keep at it and watch your stress levels decrease and your self-esteem sky rocket.

Believe in your infinite levels of

BADASSERY.

LISTEN MORE

Disagreements are one of our biggest sources of stress, but they don't have to be. Next time someone raises an issue they have with you, try to avoid a knee-jerk reaction where you immediately try to argue them down. Instead, step back and really listen. Try not to get angry but give time to consider their point of view and try to see their opinion as equal but different instead of "wrong". This sort of approach will allow you to keep your cool and avoid getting stressed.

RIGHT NOW I'D LIKE
ALL MY TROUBLES TO
STAND IN FRONT OF ME
IN A STRAIGHT LINE, AND
ONE BY ONE I'D GIVE
EACH A BLACK EYE.

SHANNON HALE

RECIPROCATE

Don't run yourself ragged putting all the energy into a relationship. If someone's giving you lukewarm vibes, reciprocate. Make time for people who make time for you. If the feeling's mutual, the energy will be equal.

Everyone's got stuff going on, so some relationships will naturally ebb and flow. If someone leaves your life, let them go: they're not your people. Focus instead on the positive, reciprocal relationships you already have, and be open to new ones too!

TAKE THINGS

ONE STEP
AT A TIME.

STOP DOING THINGS YOU F*CKING HATE

Saying no can be stressful: what if this opportunity never comes around again? What if they think I'm lazy? What if I offend someone? Stop. Invitations are not demands, and they can always be declined. Learn how to say no with kindness. If the word itself feels too harsh, try these:

- "That won't be possible."
- "I can't right now."
- "Thank you for thinking of me, but no."

Ration your yeses and your noes by checking in with yourself before you take on anything new. Being picky about what you give your energy and attention to only leads to a calmer, more fulfilling life, with more time for things you actually want to do.

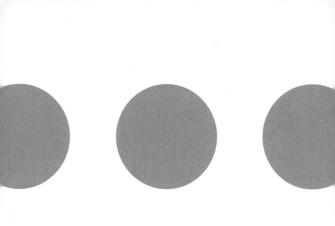

**DON'T SAY MAYBE IF
YOU WANT TO SAY NO.**

PAULO COELHO

Ignore imposter syndrome

Don't let your inner critic talk you out of opportunities. Aim high. The worst that can happen is getting turned down – which you are strong enough to cope with. If you never try, the answer will always be no.

If there's something you really want to do, don't wait for permission, don't wait until you feel 110 per cent qualified, don't worry about what-ifs... go for it, say f*ck yes!

YOU'RE A F*CKING HERO.

STOP FOR ONE F*CKING SECOND

Taking care of yourself is your most important job, so if you feel the need to pare your responsibilities back in order to recharge, do it. You can take a break any time for a second, a minute, an hour or a week. The world won't end. You will make up the time.

Take time to fill yourself up with peaceful activities that restore your energy and enthusiasm, making you feel calm, rested and ready for anything.

ONE OF THE
SYMPTOMS OF
AN APPROACHING
NERVOUS
BREAKDOWN IS
THE BELIEF THAT
ONE'S WORK
IS TERRIBLY
IMPORTANT.

BERTRAND RUSSELL

Breathe

In times of stress, your breath is always there. Focus on breathing for just a minute and see your stress levels drop and your sense of clarity return:

- Breathe in through your nose to the count of five.
- Breathe out through your mouth, gently engaging your abdominal muscles to squeeze all the breath slowly out.
- Concentrate a little harder this time – in through your nose.
- Out through your mouth.
- Close your eyes and repeat.

Take a moment to take three deep breaths whenever you feel the need to reset.

Get to know your mind and know when it's up to its old tricks

Becoming self-aware can be uncomfortable, but it's so worth it. Once you recognize the ways in which you've learned to protect your sensitive inner self, you can cultivate a more mindful attitude to your thoughts, emotions and actions.

You might choose to write in a journal or try relaxation therapy, both will help make sense of your thoughts. You'll find you can observe how your mind works – what are your deep beliefs about yourself, what are your patterns of unhealthy behaviour? Try meditating regularly to practise getting a bit of distance between you and your thoughts.

HOW BEAUTIFUL
IT IS TO DO NOTHING,
AND THEN TO REST
AFTERWARD.

SPANISH PROVERB

WEAR WHATEVER THE F*CK YOU WANT

Wear clothes that make you feel comfortable and fabulous. We all feel the pressure to look a certain way, so it takes courage to stay true to yourself wardrobe-wise. It can be stressful to try and keep up with how everyone else is dressing, so try letting go of the need to follow trends and cultivate your own look. The secret to great style is the inner confidence found when wearing clothes you love, be they simple or extravagant, expensive or basic.

Wearing something you're not comfortable in – whether it's the fit, the style or the occasion that makes you feel awkward – adds a heap of unnecessary stress to your day.

Take a moment before you leave the house to ask yourself: do I feel comfortable? If the answer is no, go change into something that's more you.

BREAK IT DOWN

Breaking tasks down into manageable chunks helps you plan how and when you will do each part. Work through each methodically, setting a timer for 20–30 minutes. When the time's up, take a short break to stretch your legs, make a drink or go outside.

This method of time-management, known as the Pomodoro Technique, boosts your concentration and productivity as well as lowering stress. The length of each "Pomodoro" is in-tune with the human attention span, and the regular breaks mean your mind can rest, reset and start afresh with the next task.

THINK

like a queen. A queen is

NOT AFRAID

to fail. Failure is another

STEPPING

stone to

GREATNESS.

OPRAH WINFREY

LOOK AT THE STARS

Try gazing up at the cosmos once in a while and contemplating your own smallness. Consider how long it has taken for the starlight to reach your eyes, and how many miles it has travelled to be there.

Studies have found that looking at the night sky significantly reduces stress levels and improves mood. It's one of nature's most awe-inspiring sights and, on a clear night, it's available to anyone, anywhere – all you need to do is look up.

THIS
TOO
SHALL
PASS.

I think best in a hot bath,
with my head tilted back
and my feet up high.

ELIZABETH JANE HOWARD

Hugging is possibly the most comforting thing in the universe. In times of stress, this wordless connection with another human being lowers your heart rate and calms your body's natural stress responses, meaning the pressures of real life can be forgotten while you're in your hug-bubble.

It's all about the feelings of safety and social support that hugging brings. When you're reminded that you're loved and supported by those around you, your brain releases a surge of feel-good hormones. Try upping your daily hug count by offering them to your friends and family more often.

HUG IT OUT

START BY DOING WHAT'S NECESSARY, THEN DO WHAT'S POSSIBLE; AND SUDDENLY: YOU ARE DOING THE IMPOSSIBLE.

ANONYMOUS

Learn from your failures

Never waste valuable mistakes by not learning from them. Take responsibility, apologize if it's warranted, and really look at your choices.

Try asking yourself the following questions:

* What was successful?
* What failed?
* How could I choose differently next time?
* Who could I learn from?

Allow yourself to feel whatever the failure brings up for you – frustration, sadness, disappointment... but don't wallow too long. Try a breathing exercise (like the one on page 81), let it go and move forward.

ACCEPT

the things you cannot change.

STOP PROCRASTINATING

Procrastination is the enemy of productivity and it can send your stress levels through the roof when you realize how much time you've wasted avoiding important tasks.

Try these anti-procrastination tools:

- Apps like Procraster and AntiSocial block internet-based distractions and help you understand your procrastination habits.
- Promise yourself a reward for completing a task – like 10 minutes on social media for an hour's work.
- Team up with a fellow procrastinator friend and work together. Having someone there to witness your work habits will keep both of you accountable and motivated.

Once you've got yourself back on track you'll feel satisfied, capable and ready to kick your to-do list's ass.

YOU ARE VALUABLE JUST
BECAUSE YOU EXIST.
NOT BECAUSE OF WHAT
YOU DO OR WHAT YOU
HAVE DONE, BUT SIMPLY
BECAUSE YOU ARE.

MAX LUCADO

QUIT COMPLAINING

Venting your frustration is good and necessary, but it's easy to slip into rumination, resentment and other general sh*ttiness when complaining becomes a way of life.

Challenge yourself to go a week without complaining – by refusing to give your attention to the things that irritate or exasperate you, you'll reduce your stress levels and feel so much more positive. If something annoying or upsetting happens, try to focus on problem-solving and learning from it, rather than assigning blame or ruminating over the details.

UN-
CLENCH.

F*ck the haters

The best people offer constructive, useful criticism with love. They help us to grow and become a better version of ourselves. But haters are a different story.

They nit-pick and undermine, offer backhanded compliments and know just how to stress you out to get a reaction.

If someone tries to tear you down, use it as motivation to prove them wrong. You are only limited by your own imagination, so don't believe people who tell you lies about yourself. Take a step back, let go of their judgements and set boundaries to keep them as close or as far away as you're comfortable with.

It's important to make sure your decisions come from a place of self-love, rather than spite – but do use their negativity as fuel to achieve your goals. Thriving while giving haters zero attention is the best revenge.

TRUST THYSELF: EVERY HEART VIBRATES TO THAT IRON STRING.

What you put in, you get out

Our minds are influenced by everything we feed them, so feed yours well! Read, watch and listen exclusively to positive, inspiring things you love. Treat your downtime as sacred and be picky about what you consume.

Put down that mediocre book, skip any song that doesn't make you wanna sing along and stop watching that boring-ass Netflix series.

Constant doom-laden news updates and a social media feed full of posts that make you feel inadequate will stress you out just as surely as stuff actually happening in your own life will.

You are

TOUGHER

*than you
look and*

BRAVER

than you know.

TAKE A BATH

There's not much that can't be improved by a hot bath. Chuck in a bath bomb, essential oil and light a few candles and you've got yourself a guaranteed stress-free zone.

As well as getting you all sparkling clean and relaxed, baths boost circulation, improve sleep and lower blood pressure. Regular bathing helps strengthen and synchronize your body's circadian rhythms (which control fluctuations in mood and behaviour throughout the day) leading to decreased stress levels and improved mood.

Try committing to one proper soak in the tub every week – sprinkle in a handful of bath salts to further relax your muscles and detoxify your skin.

To achieve great things,

TWO THINGS

are needed:

A PLAN

and not quite enough

TIME.

LEONARD BERNSTEIN

HAVE AN ORGASM

It's fun, free and healthy, you can do it alone and there's (usually) no special equipment needed. Having an orgasm triggers your brain to release loads of the stress-relieving hormone oxytocin, making you feel calm, content and relaxed.

Studies have shown that regular orgasms lead to better circulation, digestion, immunity and sleep patterns... there's even a theory that they make you more beautiful! Treating yourself to an orgasm could be the cheapest, easiest and most fun way to tell stress to f*ck off.

REMEMBER

TO
PRIORITIZE
YOUR OWN
WELL-BEING.

F*CK CAFFEINE

A lot of us are addicted to caffeine. Found in energy drinks and other fizzy drinks, as well as tea and coffee, the energy rush from caffeine helps get you out of bed in the morning but it also raises your levels of the stress hormone cortisol and heightens adrenaline... leading to the inevitable crash later on. Yikes! But once you're hooked, cutting out caffeine altogether can cause headaches, irritability, fatigue... and cold turkey can be intense.

If you feel jittery after caffeine and sluggish without it, try reducing your intake gradually – by as little as ¼ of a cup per day, or by mixing decaf into your usual blend – and see if you notice the difference. The less caffeine you drink, the smoother and more sustainable your energy levels will become, helping you lead a less stressful life.

THE ROAD TO
SUCCESS IS
ALWAYS UNDER
CONSTRUCTION.

LILY TOMLIN

EACH STEP

TAKES YOU
CLOSER

TO WHERE
YOU WANT
TO BE.

Stretch

When you release tension in your body, mental tension lessens too, helping you feel relaxed and refreshed.

Try these stretches any time you feel tense or unfocused:

- Standing up, reach upward with your right arm, and look down to your left hand that is by your side – now swap sides. Feel the stretch in your neck and along your shoulder blades.
- Sitting in a chair or on the floor, stick your legs out in front of you. Slowly point and flex your feet, enjoying the stretch along your calves.
- Raise your right arm over your head and place your right hand between your shoulder blades. Bring your left hand up behind your back to meet it. If you can, let your fingers catch each other and gently bring your right elbow backward. Relax into the stretch for a few breaths, then swap sides.

SCREW YOU,

NEGATIVITY.

SCHEDULE IN SELF-CARE

If you struggle to give yourself the downtime you need and deserve, try putting it in your diary like you would any other responsibility. That way, you'll be less likely to sideline self-care for other events, and the things you need to stay happy and relaxed don't get relegated to being just an afterthought.

Self-care is different for everyone – so the following is just a guide. Try committing to something sociable, something restful and something healthy. Perhaps one date with a friend per week, one book chapter per day and one glass of water per meal.

It is not a daily increase,
but a daily decrease. Hack
away at the inessentials.

BRUCE LEE

WALK IT OFF

Going for a walk is therapeutic as well as being free. Walking away from what's causing you stress is very tempting, and here's your permission to do it.

Walking eases tension in your muscles and puts physical distance between you and the stressful environment. If you walk mindfully – that is, using all your senses to experience your surroundings – it'll get you out of your head too. Pick a quiet, green space and pay attention to the sound of the wind, the detail of a tree's bark or the softness of a patch of moss.

While you will eventually have to return to the real world in all its stressy glory, a walking break will leave you calm, refreshed and ready to tackle almost anything.

Don't stew on negative thoughts;

LET THEM GO.

Enjoy a change of scenery

When you're feeling stressed out, uninspired and unproductive, change your environment to refresh your creativity.

Moving across the room, to a café or library, or even investing in a standing desk can change your perspective and give you a more positive outlook. If that's not an option for you, tidying or rearranging the items on your desk can have a similar effect. Improving your environment even in this seemingly small way serves as a creative outlet – as having a positive impact on your surroundings brings a sense of well-being.

Change your workspace up as soon as you feel stress or procrastination creeping in.

THE GREATEST MISTAKE YOU CAN MAKE IN LIFE IS TO BE CONTINUALLY FEARING YOU WILL MAKE ONE.

ELBERT HUBBARD

THE GRASS

IS GREENER WHERE YOU WATER IT.

Tune in, chill out

Listen to an audiobook, podcast or guided meditation when you're travelling or doing household chores. It's a great way to make "dead time" that bit more relaxing and productive.

Having something soothing or entertaining to listen to will make the time pass more quickly, and it'll mean you're more tolerant of any outside irritations that might otherwise get your blood pressure rising.

DON'T TAKE YOURSELF TOO SERIOUSLY.

Get grateful

Instead of running through your to-do list when you wake up in the morning, try getting in the habit of naming three things you're grateful for. It can be anything – the sunrise, your comfy pyjamas, the cute barista you buy your coffee from... whatever springs to mind and makes you happy to be living your life right now. You could write them in a gratitude journal or simply think about them and enjoy the feeling of gratitude.

Practising gratitude re-trains the mind to seek out and focus on the positive. Studies show that a gratitude habit decreases stress and anxiety, improves sleep and makes you more compassionate to yourself and others.

STRESS IS CAUSED
BY BEING "HERE"
BUT WANTING TO
BE "THERE".

ECKHART TOLLE

CUT DOWN ON SOCIAL MEDIA

Scrolling through pictures of our friends', acquaintances', and celebrities' seemingly perfect (but also #relatable) lives – it's addictive, entertaining... and stressful.

Scientific research is starting to show how our minds are affected by social media. Effects include herd mentality, a dependence on outside validation, shorter attention spans, lower self-esteem and the stress that comes from constant comparison with others.

While social media does have its redeeming features – keeping in touch, making us lol and even making money for some of us – it's a good idea to ration your intake.

Try dedicating a specific time each day to checking your accounts. Turn off push notifications, log out at the end of each session and for the love of all that is holy, unfollow accounts that make you feel sh*tty about yourself.

Let your shoulders drop, unclench your jaw,

BREATHE.

Let go of the past

We all have things in our past that have shaped us. Regrets, loss, grief and heartbreak are incredibly painful, and forgetting is usually not an option. Difficult emotions teamed with cultural pressure to "get over it" mean stress is piled on top of grief, making it even harder to deal with. But it is possible to make peace with your past by letting it go.

This takes time – how much time is totally personal and there's no shame in taking as much of it as you need. Everyone holds on for longer than they outwardly let on. Try writing what you're ready to let go of on a scrap of paper and burning it, or visualize walking away from painful memories. The important thing is to learn from your experiences, feel your painful emotions fully, and then let them go.

MANY A CALM RIVER BEGINS AS A TURBULENT WATERFALL, YET NONE HURTLES AND FOAMS ALL THE WAY TO THE SEA.

MIKHAIL LERMONTOV

STOP TRYING TO PLEASE EVERYBODY

People pleasing is an easy habit to get into. It feels good to be liked, and to do things for others. But it can quickly turn into an unhealthy and stressful situation for you. Taking on more than you can handle will stress you out and mean you end up neglecting yourself in favour of other people. On top of that, over-committing yourself could mean you're spread too thinly to help anyway!

Next time you feel the impulse to offer your time, energy or money to someone else, pause. Take a moment alone to consider whether you have the personal resources to offer help at this time, and what is motivating you – if it's guilt or fear of rejection, don't offer your help.

Putting yourself first might feel uncomfortable at first, but practise, practise, practise and eventually it will become second nature.

STOP

[ ]

GIVING AWAY SO
MANY OF YOUR
PRECIOUS F*CKS.

Respond in your own time

Not everything requires an immediate response from you. If you're feeling overwhelmed or you're simply too busy, you can ignore or delay your response to an email or text until a more convenient time for you.

If you're worried you'll forget to reply, try using the snooze feature, setting yourself a reminder or setting aside time each day for catching up with messages.

Even if someone is speaking directly to you, don't be pressured into giving an answer you feel rushed into. A simple phrase like "let me think about it and get back to you" will politely excuse you from the conversation, giving you time and space to respond when you're ready.

I AM NOT AFRAID
OF STORMS, FOR I
AM LEARNING HOW
TO SAIL MY SHIP.

LOUISA MAY ALCOTT

DIVE IN

Wild swimming – swimming outdoors in lidos, lakes, rivers and the sea – is known to ease depression, tension and fatigue. It's thought the physical stress of plunging into cold water improves our ability to cope with other kinds of physical and emotional stress. Coupled with the fresh air and exercise that come with wild swimming, it's a bit of an all-rounder when it comes to beating stress and looking after your mental well-being. Who knew freezing your ass off in the great outdoors could be so beneficial!

(Always make sure you're swimming somewhere suitable and read up on how to keep safe in the water before you take the plunge.)

YOU DO NOT EXIST FOR OTHERS' CONVENIENCE.

Let go of tension

You've probably come across stress balls before – the idea behind squeezing a firm, squidge-able object to counteract stress is all about tension. The act of squeezing tenses the muscles and releasing this tension releases both mental and physical stress, bringing you back to a state of relaxation.

Using the same principle, you can make yourself a human stress ball. Try working your way down your body, tensing and relaxing your muscles – start by making your scrunchiest, angriest face… then relax all your facial muscles. Next clench your shoulders right up to your ears… and let them go. Move on to your abdominal muscles, your glutes, leg muscles and finally your toes. You'll end up feeling relaxed from head to toe.

Life is

TEN
PER CENT

what you experience and

NINETY
PER CENT

how you respond to it.

STEVE MARABOLI

THE 5-MINUTE RULE

No, this isn't about food that's been dropped on the floor. This is about those tiny little jobs that are oh so easy to ignore and put off, until you have several hundred tiny little jobs and one big feeling of stress.

So, the 5-minute rule: if something will take less than 5 minutes to complete, do it immediately. Take out the trash, post that letter and book that appointment! Don't skim over them on your to-do list or ignore them when you pass by. Get in the habit of doing the little things as they arise, and you'll find your life becomes much less stressful and better organized.

Your

BEST

is enough.

F*ck alcohol

There's nothing like cracking open a cold bottle of beer after a stressful day, and the consumption of moderate amounts of alcohol has been found to be beneficial in regulating stress.

But while alcohol gives us a bit of temporary relief, too much of it can make things worse. Habitual drinking raises levels of cortisol, making you jumpy and anxious as well as altering the brain's chemistry and makes you less able to cope with stressful situations.

If you want to cut down on drinking, try taking a month off or alternating soft drinks and alcoholic ones on a night out. If you like a few drinks to relax in social situations, swap the bar for an activity like bowling or a games night to break the ice. For a replacement stress-reliever, try a short burst of intense, high-energy exercise like running, boxercise or cycling.

Power for me is "no"... That's when you know your worth, when you know your value.

TARAJI P. HENSON

ROLL

WITH THE
PUNCHES.

SWAP "I HAVE TO" FOR "I GET TO"

Think back to a time when you dreamed of the things you have now. Try imagining 10-year-old you – what about your life today would impress that kid?

Consider how lucky you are to have the responsibilities you do. It might not feel that way sometimes, when you have to drag yourself out of bed for work or take your dog for a walk when it's p*ssing it down.

If those are your problems... you have a job – excellent! And you have a dog that thinks you're the greatest – you lucky thing!

You have the power to change your perception by choosing a positive outlook on the things you do.

FAILURE IS A BEGINNING, NOT THE END.

CUT YOURSELF SOME SLACK

We are often our own harshest critics, holding ourselves to a far higher standard than we do the rest of the human race.

Next time you catch your inner critic judging you, ask whether you would speak to a friend in that way. Try extending the compassion and understanding you give so freely to your friends, to yourself.

IMPERFECTION IS NOT OUR PERSONAL PROBLEM — IT IS A NATURAL PART OF EXISTING.

TARA BRACH

TRY JOURNALING

Keeping a notebook handy for journaling your thoughts is a brilliant stress-reliever – it's been found to improve sleep, memory and general mood. There's no need to be entertaining or funny, or even to make sense. The only person who'll read your journal is you.

If you're not sure where to start, try having a good old rant about what's stressing you out. Once you've expressed some of that anger and frustration, you'll feel more able to cope with the situation and it'll be easier to see solutions more clearly.

Adulting
like a

BOSS.

THE DIFFERENCE BETWEEN SUCCESSFUL PEOPLE AND REALLY SUCCESSFUL PEOPLE IS THAT REALLY SUCCESSFUL PEOPLE SAY NO TO ALMOST EVERYTHING.

WARREN BUFFETT

GET GROUNDED

Connecting with the Earth has been found to reduce stress and tension, slow your heart rate and give you a better night's sleep. Thanks to the slight negative charge of the Earth's surface, placing your bare skin on grass, sand, soil or in a body of natural water has a calming effect on the body's central nervous system.

Next time you're out in nature – or even just in your own back garden – try going barefoot for 15 minutes to see if you can feel the difference. Try and schedule in a bit of barefoot time to ground yourself every week.

WITHIN YOU, THERE
IS A STILLNESS AND A
SANCTUARY TO WHICH
YOU CAN RETREAT AT ANY
TIME AND BE YOURSELF.

HERMANN HESSE

Get out of your head and into your senses

If your thoughts are exhausting right now and you need a break, try this simple mindfulness exercise. Notice one thing you can see. One thing you can hear. One thing you can smell. One thing you can taste. And one thing you can feel.

Paying attention to your senses rather than your thoughts will bring you into the present moment and help break negative thought cycles.

BECOME

[

]

UNF*CKWITHABLE.

Counterintuitive stress hacks

Give stress the middle finger by doing the opposite of what it wants you to do.

- If you feel financial pressure ➜ donate a little money or time to a deserving cause
- If you feel stressed about your appearance ➜ take a selfie
- If you feel time pressure ➜ do something unproductive, like taking a walk
- If you feel overwhelmed at work ➜ do some housework
- If you feel rushed into a decision ➜ step away and take time alone to think
- If you feel unsupported ➜ help out a friend

Sometimes the antidote to stress is to simply stop playing by its rules.

ONCE WE BELIEVE
IN OURSELVES,
WE CAN RISK
CURIOSITY, WONDER,
SPONTANEOUS
DELIGHT, OR ANY
EXPERIENCE THAT
REVEALS THE
HUMAN SPIRIT.

E. E. CUMMINGS

LOVE YOURSELF

This is the key to leading a calm and happy life. When you love yourself, you trust yourself and your ability to cope with whatever life throws at you.

Start with something you already love or like about yourself. It can be anything – your hair, your taste in music, your encyclopaedic knowledge of *Friends* episodes. Acknowledge, appreciate and nurture that thing as often as you can, then add something else. For example, if you love your passion for learning, take an online course or pass on something you've learned to others.

Once you start, you'll learn to love every part of yourself – every body part, every emotion and every habit.

Love yourself so much that when something stresses you out, you can trust your own strength and judgement to handle the situation and balance your own well-being at the same time.

BE GENTLE

WITH
YOURSELF.

Muddy

WATER

let

STAND

becomes

CLEAR.

LAO TZU

GO TO YOUR DOCTOR

If stress feels overwhelming and it's starting to affect your sleep, mood or relationships, it might be time to talk to a doctor or therapist.

Asking for help when your mental health is suffering is a sign of strength and an important part of valuing and looking after yourself. You deserve to live a peaceful, happy life – do what it takes to get there.

Make happiness your

PRIORITY.

If you're interested in finding out more about our books, find us on Facebook at Summersdale Publishers and follow us on Twitter at @Summersdale.

www.summersdale.com